BOLSHEVISM

BOLSHEVISM

HENRY WILLIAM LEE,
WILL THORNE

ISBN: 978-93-5420-721-1

Published: 1919

LECTOR HOUSE LLP
E-MAIL: lectorpublishing@gmail.com

BOLSHEVISM
A CURSE & DANGER TO THE WORKERS

BY

H. W. LEE

(Editor of "Justice"; Author of "The First of May: International Labour Day"; "A Socialist View of the Unemployed Question"; "Social-Democracy and the Zollverein"; "The Triumph of the Trust under Free Trade"; "The Great Strike Movement of 1911"; and "Why Starve? Britain's Food in War—and in Peace.").

WITH FOREWORD BY
WILL THORNE, M.P.

SECOND EDITION.

1919.

FOREWORD
BY WILL THORNE, M.P.

I have been asked to write a brief introduction to the pamphlet which my old friend and comrade H.W. Lee has written on the undercurrent of Bolshevist propaganda going on in this country, of which the recent unauthorised strike outbreaks are outward and visible signs. I do this gladly. Our comrade Lee, through being long associated with the Social-Democratic Federation as its Secretary, and his editorship of "Justice" during the last five years, has gained a knowledge of International Socialist movements in their many phases which renders his pamphlet both authoritative and reliable.

I hope the pamphlet will have a wide circulation in all the large industrial centres, because I feel convinced that the majority of the rank and file of the wage-earners do not and cannot know what it is that our Bolshevists are striving for. They have not the faintest idea in what direction some of them are being led. The Bolshevists in certain industrial centres want to impose their own authority on the rank and file of the workers, using catch-words for that purpose. If they succeed in this direction they will set to work to undermine the trade union movement of this country, and upset, instead of making use of, the means we at present possess for improving our economic conditions.

Our minds go back to the Leeds "Convention," held in June, 1917. The delegates at that Conference declared that they were in favour of Workmen's and Soldiers' Councils being formed in all the large industrial centres of the country. Nothing whatever came of it. But the W.S.C.s then controlling the revolutionary undercurrent in Russia were totally different from the Bolshevist tyranny of to-day, and many of the delegates who formed the W.S.C.s in various parts of Russia after the Revolution have been imprisoned or shot because they opposed the domination of Lenin and Trotzky.

Last Tuesday I saw two friends whom I met in Petrograd in April, 1917, and both of them absolutely confirm the statements made in the Press about the hundreds of men and women who have been shot without any trial or confirmation of the charges brought against them.

An article which appears in the "Nineteenth Century" of January, written by Mr. Pierson, who was imprisoned in the Fortress of St. Peter and St. Paul last October, after being arrested at the British Embassy in Petrograd at the same time that Captain Cromie was shot, also confirms the brutalities that are taking place constantly in Petrograd and other parts of Russia.

A letter in the "Daily Express," written by Colonel John Ward, M.P., shows the terrible hell which Bolshevism is making, and the methods that are being pursued by the followers of Lenin and Trotzky. If the Soldiers' and Workmen's Councils had done their duty in the latter part of April, 1917, after Lenin made his two hours' speech in the Duma on April 17, they would have sent him back whence he came, because it is a well-known fact that he was allowed to pass through Germany with thirty other companions in a first-class saloon. I am quite convinced that it was not the Russian people who were paying his expenses during the time he was carrying on his pernicious propaganda work in various parts of Russia. The downfall of the Soldiers' and Workmen's Councils has been the consequence of their giving Lenin and his thirty companions full freedom to spread their anarchical creed and the wiping out of duly elected Assemblies.

The leading men of the Bolshevik movement in this country are out for the overthrow of things as they are by physical force as soon as they feel confident that they have a good number of the rank and file of the wage-earners behind them. I want to warn the wage-earners—men and women of my own class—against being associated with such people, because I know that their tactics cannot remedy the economic and industrial injustices under which the industrial workers are suffering. They can be rectified by Social-Democratic education, scientific organisation in the trade union movement, and by using political powers to that end.

The methods adopted by the unauthorised shop stewards movement in the different parts of the country must be rigorously suppressed, and properly appointed shop stewards and works committees in all factories and workshops must be elected instead. By that method industrial and economic improvements can be brought about with the greatest benefit and the least harm to all.

The pamphlet gives a very clear statement about what is taking place in connection with the Bolshevist movement. That is the reason why I trust that it will have a wide circulation in all the large industrial centres of the country.

WILL THORNE.

February 13, 1919.

"BOLSHEVISM"

Russia has given most countries of the world a new word. "Bolshevism" is to-day known universally, though its meaning is not by any means so universal. In Russia it has a very definite and often striking meaning, as many anti-Bolsheviks have known and are learning to their cost. Elsewhere it has a wider, if looser, significance, and is frequently employed to express or describe a number of things to which one objects. Our own Press, for instance, flings "Bolshevik" and "Bolshevism" at everybody and everything that it denounces, or against whom and which it seeks to raise prejudice. In this respect it has often overreached itself, for it is causing some to accept the Russian Bolsheviks at their own estimation, because they know that many of the things styled "Bolshevist" are not as bad as they are made out to be.

In Russia "Bolshevik" means majority, and "Menshevik" minority. Their real significance was purely an internal one for the Russian Social-Democratic Party. It is important to make this point clear, for now and again we come across British supporters of and sympathisers with the Russian Bolsheviks who take the name as a proof that the Government of Lenin and Trotzky actually represents the majority of the Russian people! Nothing is more contrary to the fact. The Bolshevist "coup de rue" of November, 1917, was as complete a usurpation of power as that of Louis Napoleon in 1851. True it was a usurpation by professed Socialists, supposedly in the interests of the Russian working class, but it was no less a usurpation and an attack on democracy which only success in the interests of the Russian working class could possibly justify. The forcible dissolution of the Constituent Assembly by the Bolsheviks two months afterwards, because the elections did not go in their favour, compelled them to take the road to complete domination, and they are now unable to retrace their steps, even if, as is reported, the more honest of them wish to do so.

BOLSHEVIKS, MENSHEVIKS, AND SOCIAL REVOLUTIONARIES.

The terms "Bolshevik" and "Menshevik" (majority and minority) arose from the division in the Russian Social-Democracy which had shown itself at the Congress held in London in 1903. The difference is generally assumed to be one of tactics—of a readiness to co-operate with other parties for certain definite objects under certain special conditions ("Menshevik"), or of complete antagonism and opposition to all other parties every time and all the time ("Bolshevik"). But the difference lies deeper than that. "Bolshevism" is, in effect, the Russian form of "impossibilism." From this the thorough-going Social-Democrats of all countries have to suffer at times. By divorcing the application of Socialist principles and measures from the actual life of the day, and arguing and discussing "in vacuo," impossibilism drives many, who see the utter sterility of its results, into the opposite direction, that of opportunism for the moment without much thought for the future.

Until their "coup de rue" of November, 1917, the Russian Bolsheviks regarded themselves as the extreme Left of the Russian Social-Democratic Party. But latterly they have dropped the name Social-Democrat—so much the better for Social-Democracy—and have adopted that of the "Russian Communist Party"—so much the worse for Communism, for towards Communism the Social-Democratic Commonwealths of the future are bound to tend. "Bolshevism" to-day, where it is honest, is in the main a revival of the Anarchism of Bakunine, together with a policy of armed insurrection, and a seizure of political power which shall install the "dictatorship of the proletariat." That is the dividing line between the Bolsheviks and their Social-Democratic opponents, the Mensheviks, and their far more numerous and powerful antagonists, the Social Revolutionaries, who obtained an overwhelming majority in the Constituent Assembly which the Bolsheviks dissolved by force. The Social Revolutionaries seek the emancipation of the peasants and workers by democratic means—the only safe and sure way—though they were quite ready to use force for the overthrow of Tsardom, happily effected in March, 1917. Unhappily, though, Bolshevik terrorism, with its complete inability to carry out its promises of "peace and bread" for the Russian people, and certain European financial interests are together rehabilitating reaction in Russia, and the people and the peasants may be driven to put up with some new autocratic régime in the hope that it may shield them from the present terrorism and secure them something to eat.

BOLSHEVIST INTOLERANCE.

Innumerable instances could be given of the bitter intolerance of the honest Bolshevik fanatics towards all sections of the International Socialist movement with which they have not agreed. Paul Axelrod, one of the founders of Russian Social-Democracy, in a pamphlet published at Zürich in 1915, entitled "The Crisis and the Duties of International Social-Democracy," reproaches Lenin with seeking to carry into the internal struggles of the Socialist Parties in Europe "specifically Russian methods" which aim directly at creating troubles and divisions, and branding without any distinction "nearly all the known and respected bodies of International Social-Democracy as traitors and deserters stranded in the bourgeois camp, treating these comrades, whose international conscience and sentiments are above all suspicion, as National Liberals, chauvinists, philistines, traitors, etc." Is this the way in which to raise the enthusiasm of the workers for the cause of Socialism? Is this the manner in which the spirit of self-sacrifice can be roused in the masses? It savours far too much of the old implacable bitterness of the Terrorists—reasonable and natural enough in their secret conspiracies, where a fellow-conspirator might be a police agent—but utterly out of place and mischievous when introduced into open propaganda and organisation.

To this jaundiced outlook of the prominent Bolsheviks is added ignorance of administration. Nearly all of them are refugees who have spent many years of their lives outside of Russia. They have evolved theories of Socialist policy from their inner consciousness without an opportunity of putting them to practical tests—until now, when the world is in the throes of a war crisis. And they attempt to apply their theories of the "dictatorship of the proletariat" in a vast nation made up of various races in different stages of civilisation, only just entering upon full capitalist development, where the proletariat, the wage workers, constitute fewer than 20,000,000 out of a total population of 180,000,000! And yet there are supporters of the Bolsheviks in Britain who profess to be Marxists—more Marxist than Marx, in fact—and who can countenance such a logical outrage on the "materialist conception of history"!

OFFENSIVE AND DEFENSIVE WARS.

Nothing better illustrates the unreality of some of Lenin's theories than his attitude on national self-defence. In 1915 he and Zinovieff, another well-known Bolshevik, published a pamphlet on "Socialism and the War." One chapter dealt with "A War of Defence and a War of Attack." It contains this passage:—"If to-morrow, for example, Morocco were to go to war against France, the Indies against England, and China against Russia, they would be wars of defence, just wars, independently of any question of which began the war." Being "wars of defence, just wars," the people would obviously be justified in taking part in them from Lenin's point of view. Now let us see where the logic of this contention will land us. Morocco, possibly because what capitalism is there is foreign, may justly wage war against France; but if France fights a war of defence against an aggressive attack by Germany, she is engaged in an "imperialist war." Similarly, if India rises against Britain, the people will be fighting a just war; but if Britain supports France and Belgium against German imperialism, she is carrying on an "imperialist war." Hence it follows that, if the Central Powers had won the war, and Belgium had been subjugated by Germany, Belgium would have been fully justified in fighting to recover her independence; but in defending that independence which she would have a right to recover, if deprived of it, she was taking part in an "imperialist war "! Such is Leninist logic when brought down to actual facts.

In short, Lenin, like Bakunine, loves ideas more than men. This may be said of all the honest Bolshevist fanatics. There are others—many of them. And even the genuine fanatics appear to have reached a stage of mental "impossibilism" where the end not only justifies the means, but any means must necessarily help to achieve the end.

We know the Bolsheviks were conveyed to Russia in April, 1917, via Germany in sealed carriages with the consent of the German authorities. The Swiss Bolshevik, Platten, arranged the affair with the German Government. That the German Government expected that the Bolshevist mission to Russia would be of advantage to Germany cannot be questioned; otherwise the Bolshevist refugees would not have been allowed to go to Petrograd through Germany. The Bolsheviks themselves knew that their actions in the Russian Revolution would help Imperialist Germany, for the "Berner Tagwacht" announced, after they had left Switzerland, that they were "perfectly well aware that the German Government is only permitting the transit of those persons because it believes that their presence in Russia will strengthen the anti-war tendencies there." It is the same with whatever money was supplied by Germany to the Bolsheviks. It would all help to establish the "dictatorship of the proletariat."

It is necessary to refer also to Leo Trotzky. Some who are convinced of Lenin's honesty of purpose do not hold the same view of Trotzky. Lenin is the implacable theorist in whose nostrils compromise of any sort stinks. Trotzky is not of that character. He is much more adaptable. And he has changed opinions on war issues more than once during the war. In the autumn of 1914 or the beginning of 1915, Trotzky wrote a brilliant pamphlet, "Der Krieg und die Internationale" ("The War and the International"). In that pamphlet he boldly declared that the break-up of the Austro-Hungarian Empire was a necessity. While ridiculing defensive wars, he nevertheless wrote: "The more obstinate the resistance of France—and now, truly, it is her duty to protect her territory and her independence against the German attack—the more surely does she hold, and will hold, the German army on the Western front." Again: "The victory of Germany over France—a very regrettable strategic necessity in the opinion of German Social-Democracy—would signify first of all not merely the defeat of the permanent army under a democratic republican régime, but the victory of the feudal and monarchical constitution over the democratic and republican constitution." Thus wrote Trotzky while still a Social-Democrat, before he became a Bolshevist dictator. How, then, can he denounce France for fighting an "imperialist war," or Britain for helping her to prevent a "victory of the feudal and monarchical constitution over the democratic and republican constitution"?

THE "DICTATORSHIP OF THE PROLETARIAT."

The "dictatorship of the proletariat" appeals to Trotzky, because he has become virtually the dictator of the proletariat and everything else in Russia within the power of the "Red Guards" and his Chinese battalions. These Chinese battalions, recruited from Chinese labourers employed behind the military lines while Russia was in the war, may be responsible for some of the "executions" which have taken place. The Bolshevist emissary, Maxim Litvinoff, pooh-poohs all stories of massacres. It is generally the dregs of the Chinese population who are recruited for labour gangs abroad; and if "removals" of "counter-revolutionaries" can be accomplished by Chinese battalions, the Bolsheviks can then aver that they have not had a hand in it! Since the acceptance of the Brest-Litovsk Treaty because Russia could fight no longer, Trotzky has not only talked of raising Bolshevik armies, but has succeeded in raising them and officering them by officers of the old Tsarist régime. What Trotzky would not do against the German armies he is quite prepared to do against those portions of Russia that have taken advantage of the self-determination granted by the Bolshevist Administration. Perhaps the peculiar Bolshevist philosophy regarding wars of defence is also to apply to neighbouring States if they do not happen to be strong militarily. You must not prevent the "self-determination" of any portion of an existing State, but you may attack it when "self-determined," in the interests of the "international Social Revolution" and the "dictatorship of the proletariat." That sort of action, when undertaken by an autocracy, is usually described as an act of imperialist aggression in order to divert attention from internal difficulties; and Bolshevism in Russia is an autocracy—a dictatorship not of the proletariat, but over the proletariat. It cannot possibly be anything else.

The Russian Revolution of March, 1917, was in many respects similar to the French Revolution of 1789. It brought the downfall of absolute monarchy. It was not so bourgeois in character as the French Revolution, because there was a definite proletarian class in

Russia, though small in comparison with its immense population, and capitalist production was established. But the Russian Revolution had this disadvantage compared with the French Revolution—there was practically no class able to take over the administration in the interests of the Revolution as with the French; and if that was so when certain bourgeois elements were with the Revolution, how much less of administrative knowledge would there be in a Bolshevist Government over millions of ignorant workers and peasants accustomed only to a despotic régime, whose "Commissaries" are mainly refugees, most of whom have lost all real touch with Russian internal affairs?

BOLSHEVIST INQUISITION.

There is not the slightest need to accept the capitalist Press of this or any other country as authoritative on the present condition of things in Russia. Consult the Bolshevist organs themselves, particularly the "Izvestya" and "Pravda." They give quite enough evidence to prove what terrorism prevails, how all freedom of the Press, speech and public meeting is ruthlessly suppressed. The following is from "Pravda" of October 8 last:—

> "The absence of the necessary restraint makes one feel appalled at the 'instruction' issued by the All-Russian Extraordinary Commission to 'All Provincial Extraordinary Commissions,' which says: 'The All-Russian Extraordinary Commission is perfectly independent in its work, carrying out house searches, arrests, executions, of which it *afterwards* reports to the Council of the People's Commissaries and to the Central Executive Council.' Further, the Provincial and District Extraordinary Commissions 'are independent in their activities, and when called upon by the local Executive Council present a report of their work.' In so far as house searches and arrests are concerned, a report made *afterwards* may result in putting right irregularities committed owing to lack of restraint. The same cannot be said of executions.... It can also be seen from the 'instruction' that personal safety is to a certain ex-

tent guaranteed only to members of the Government, of the Central Council and of the local Executive Committees. With the exception of these few persons, all members of the local Committees of the [Bolshevist] Party, of the Control Committees, and of the Executive Committee of the Party may be shot at any time by the decision of any Extraordinary Commission of a small district town if they happen to be on its territory, and a report of that made *afterwards*."

"Vorwärts," quoting from "Pravda," says that the Bolshevist organ reports that 13,764 persons have been executed within the last three months.

As regards the internal economic situation in Russia under Bolshevist rule, a Russian workman, whose experience has not been confined to Petrograd and Moscow, makes the following statement in the "Social-Demokraten" of Stockholm:—

"The output of the factories has decreased by 80 per cent., notwithstanding that the Revolutionary Committees stimulate production with the revolver. The condition of the railways is worse than ever. All the industrial workmen are against the Bolsheviks, and the same is the case with the peasants. The so-called 'Committees of the Poor' are drawn from the small number of peasants who sought employment in the factories during the war and have now returned to the country. The only supporters of the Bolsheviks, apart from the Letts and the Chinese, are those belonging to their own official caste. The European Press has rather understated than exaggerated the Red Terror."

As regards food conditions,[1] the Bolshevist Administration seems to be thorough and precise in the issue of food-cards of all descriptions, according to the four categories into which the population is divided. More food-cards, in fact, appear to have been issued to the population of Moscow than the population itself, which was

---

[1] Comrade "R.," who has written much for "Justice" on the food question abroad, has supplied these particulars.—H.W.L.

1,694,971 last April. Restaurants, dining-rooms, etc., are fully supplied with supplementary food-cards. But what of supplies? They are, after all, the main thing. Translated into English money and weight, the prices last September were as follows: Potatoes, 7½d. a lb.; fresh cabbage, 7d. a lb.; fish (supply diminishing), pickled herrings from 1s. 9d. to 3s. 3d. a lb.; smoked herrings, from 2s. 4d. to 4s. each; meat, 7s. 7d. a lb.; pork, 12s. 8d. a lb.; boiled sausage, 9s. 3d. a lb.; smoked sausage, 11s. 10d. a lb.; milk, of which there was little, was 2s. 6d. a bottle; cream butter, 25s. 3d. a lb.; lump sugar, 25s. 3d. a lb. In Petrograd meat was from 9s. 7d. a lb.; veal, 11s. a lb.; pork, 12s. 7d. a lb.; mutton, 10s. 1d. a lb. Fish, supplies of which were limited, were about the same prices as at Moscow. The figures of municipal bread-baking in Petrograd for last April, May and June were 328,128, 262,075 and 185,222 puds respectively. A pud is 36 lbs. This indicates a most serious reduction. According to rations on the bread-cards, which are ⅜ lb. per day, with the same amount for supplementary cards for workers' categories, and ⅛ lb. a day per child, the monthly supply for Petrograd should be 792,000 puds.

In October reports from Tambov, Viatka, Vladimir, Tula and Saratov indicate that, though supplies of all kinds of grain were fairly good, the disorganisation of transport was so great that the larger part of those supplies remained where they were. A number of delegates were sent to Saratov to obtain 30,000 puds of breadstuffs for twenty-five workmen's organisations in Moscow. They only succeeded in obtaining 3,000 puds, and they complained most bitterly of "bureaucracy" at the hands of the Saratov Provincial Food Committee, who kept them waiting a very long time and finally passed them on to a local Committee who declined to do anything. They demanded that pressure should be brought to bear on the Provincial Committee to make them disgorge part of their large reserves for the starving centre.

RUSSIAN CO-OPERATIVE SOCIETIES.

Recently reports and articles have been appearing in certain of the Labour and capitalist Press favourable to the Bolsheviks, notably the "Labour Leader," concerning the co-operative movement in Russia. It is alleged that the growth of the co-operative movement there is evidence that the Bolshevist Government is really and seriously building up a new Socialist society despite the grave difficulties within and the antagonism from without. It is true that the co-operative movement is going ahead in Russia, but it is not because of, but in spite of, Bolshevism. The co-operative movement in Russia is not the product of the Bolshevist Government; it existed and progressed under Tsardom. The help which the co-operative societies rendered to the Russian people during the war is beyond all dispute. The majority of the co-operators in the area under Bolshevist domination are forced to work with the Bolshevist Soviets in order to save their societies from dissolution. The co-operative societies in Siberia, representing two million affiliated families, a population of about ten millions, have been the backbone of the opposition to the Bolshevist Government east of the Urals.

Bolshevism in Russia is, in fact, a revival of the Anarchism of Bakunine, tinged with certain Marxist theories which the Bolshevik refugees have gathered during their numerous sojourns abroad. It is a worship of the Revolution to which everything must be sacrificed. In its adoration of the Goddess of Liberty it is willing to crush the freedom of human beings. The change from Tsardom to Bolshevism is, to use Trotzky's cynical phrase, "the turn of the wheel."

The Bolshevist Government has now dominated the central portion of European Russia for more than a twelvemonth. It bases its demand for general recognition on the fact that it has lasted a year without being overturned, and contends that that proves it has the support of "Soviet" Russia. The brief statement of internal conditions at Moscow and Petrograd made above suggests that the reports of terrible food shortage in those great cities, which come from independent sources, are not entirely destitute of foundation. And yet the apologists of the Bolsheviks here assure us that in Russia at the present time we have a "Socialist Republic of a very high order"!

These facts require to be made thoroughly well known among the working classes of these islands. The idea is being assiduously put about, more subterraneously than openly, that there is now established in Russia a genuine Socialist Republic, or, at all events, a real and conscious attempt on the part of the workers and peasants of Russia to establish such a Republic. Given this idea, there is every reason for a popular agitation to prevent anything being done by the British Government and its allies to hamper that Socialist Republic in the early stages of its development. Unfortunately, the utter incapacity of the recent and present Coalition to come to any definite policy regarding Russia, and the inclination of some of its members to back the reactionists, while standing aloof from the real democratic forces in Russia which support the Constituent Assembly, play completely into the hands of the Bolsheviks of Russia and their sympathisers here. Whatever Bolshevist undercurrents there are in the present reckless strike movements in Glasgow, Belfast and elsewhere are therefore due in great part to the Governments of Mr. Lloyd George. Nevertheless it behoves the working class of these islands to take cognisance of the facts concerning Russia, for they will enable them to realise clearly the grave mischief that these "unauthorised" strikes are doing, more to their own class and the country generally than to the capitalists against whom the efforts of the majority of the strikers are directed.

BOLSHEVISM ON THE CLYDE.

The Clyde is the centre of Bolshevism in Britain, though the spirit of it is in other parts also. But on the Clyde a number of very determined and exceedingly well meaning, but "heady," Socialists of the S.L.P. "impossibilist" type have influenced by sheer persistence a good many others who do not understand whither they are being led. Here, again, the "dictatorship of the proletariat" means the dictation of the proletariat by these "impossibilists," in order to bring capitalist industry to its knees. For that purpose strikes are to be brought about as frequently as possible on no matter what pretext, provided that pretext calls out enough "hands" to paralyse capitalist industry. It may be increased wages one day, shorter hours the next, shop conditions the day after, anything that will cause men to "down tools."

The idea, obviously, is to reduce industry to such a state of chaos that it becomes absolutely unprofitable to the employers, and thus it will be easier for the shop committees to take over the "control of industry" by Soviets from which all "bourgeois" and "counter-revolutionaries" shall be excluded. Meanwhile, when the strikes have reached a certain point, the demand shall be made for Government intervention, which, if granted under vague threats of terrible things to come, will redound to the power and credit of the Bolshevist leaders; and if not, and disturbances take place, then the leaders will be arrested, the revolutionary fires will be lighted on the Clyde, and will spread over the whole country; the leaders in question will be released from gaol by enthusiastic "revolutionary" crowds; and then will follow a glorified transformation scene as in a pantomime, with the heroes bathed in gorgeous "revolutionary" lime-light effects. I should not write in this fashion did I not know that this idea has influenced a few of the most single-minded and devoted Socialists on the Clyde, and we can only regret that such really noble spirits should have been unable to keep their heads in the greatest crisis in the world's history.

THE "DICTATORSHIP OF THE PROLETARIAT" IN OPERATION.

The battle cry of the Russian Bolsheviks and their sympathisers and would-be imitators elsewhere is the "dictatorship of the proletariat." Let us consider what that means. Dictatorship means despotism, and whether it is that of a Tsar or a Kaiser, an oligarchy or a Bolshevik administration, it is despotism—nothing more and nothing less. Impatience with the slowness of the mass of the people is only to be expected in all who see what human existence could be made on this planet, how enjoyable and pleasurable life might be made by light and pleasant labour for all, with the vast powers which man now possesses over Nature. I don't suppose there is a single Socialist who has spent twenty years of his or her life in the cause of International Social-Democracy who has not at times wished that the Social Revolution could be quickly brought about by some benevolent despotism. That a similar train of thought should have entered the minds of Russian refugees, driven from a land where political democracy in any form appeared almost hopeless of achievement, is only natural, and equally natural that it should have been pursued to its abstract logical conclusion, inasmuch as, unlike ourselves, they were not working actually amongst the people day in and day out to understand how impossible of realisation such a wish must be. Impatience with the mass—however the Mass may be worshipped—is at the bottom of the idea of the "dictatorship of the proletariat." They must be emancipated in spite of themselves. Liberty and democracy can come afterwards when the Socialist dictators have transformed capitalist society into the Socialist State. During that transformation the mass must obey the minority which has seized power; it must accept as right and just what that minority decrees; it must abandon liberty of speech and the Press, or at least it must refuse those liberties to all who do not agree with the actions of the minority in power. And if the mass don't like it, well——! Are these not precisely the principles on which Lenin and Trotzky are striving to create this "Socialist Republic of a very high order"? And are they not revealed in the attempts of a small minority to impose their will on the majority during our own strike influenza? Often is it observable that those who most vehemently denounce the slightest exercise of power in others have not the faintest objection to using it ruthlessly themselves. Bolshevism, then, is another phase, and anything but a pleasant phase, of Utopian Socialism, whatever use of the name of Karl Marx be made in connection with its advocacy.

THE BLIND SAMSON.

The wage-earners constitute by far the largest section of the community. Their votes, now more than ever, can do much to control the administration of the country if they will take the trouble to exercise that control in the direction of securing the thorough democratisation of the State, so that it may be made ready to organise the industries of the nation for the common good. The paralysis of industry will hurt the capitalist employers unquestionably, but it will certainly not benefit the workers. Blind Samson damaged the Philistines when he pulled down their temple; but he did not come out unscathed—quite the contrary. The Social Revolution—i.e., the change from capitalist production for profit to social production for use—cannot be made with rose-water; but that is no reason why there should be blood-letting just for the fun of seeing if red corpuscles are present in sufficient quantity.

Let them be what they may, the trade unions are the only form of working-class organisation to-day which can secure for the workers a decent standard of existence under capitalist conditions of industry. Anything which tends to weaken them and reduce their influence, whether in the interests of the employers or for the supposed advancement of r-r-r-revolutionary proletarian principles, whatever they may be, will be harmful to the workers. It is for the workers themselves to see that their trade unions shall be the means of securing something more than higher wages or even shorter hours of labour. War conditions have shown what a will-o'-the-wisp are mere increases of pay; and short hours of labour such as could easily be arranged under collective organisation of industry, with all the economies of effort which co-operation would effect, cannot be secured under capitalism. That surely should be obvious to all who call themselves Socialists and who have even a passing acquaintance with economics; otherwise, why the necessity of the Co-operative Commonwealth? Socialist policy towards the trade unions should be, in short, not their capture for political purposes, nor their upset for Bolshevist phantasies, but one of educating the trade unionists. It is only along that line that the Social-Democratic movement can make real and steady progress.

The policy of the strike for anything and everything is not only anti-social; it is anti-Socialist. Writing on the strike outbreak of 1911,[2] I said: "The mass strike is rarely effective, save in a negative fashion. It is successful mostly when used against some particular object or for some definite purpose of the moment. It can be used to break an objectionable agreement; it may prevent the putting into force of an unpopular law, or the passing of some tyrannical measure; it may check an attempt to suppress popular liberties, such as they are; and it may prove the best possible means of preventing war between two countries, if action in that direction be taken equally in both countries. But as *the* means for the overthrow of the capitalist system and the establishment of the Socialist Republic it is useless. Those who rely upon the general strike as *the* means for the realisation of Social-Democracy are like the ancient Gauls, of whom it is said that they shook all States and founded none."

---

[2] "The Great Strike Movement of 1911, and Its Lessons."

SPORADIC AND LIGHTNING STRIKES ANTI-SOCIAL AND ANTI-SOCIALIST.

What applied to the strike movement of 1911 applies with even greater force to the present strike ebullitions, in which the presence of Russian Bolsheviks is to be noted. This is all in accordance with the Bolshevist plan of "world revolution" for which roubles are being plentifully furnished, mainly through agents in Sweden. The prevailing idea is to pull down bourgeois society, no matter what the consequences. If conditions generally in the countries of Europe under capitalism to-day were like what they were here a century ago, coupled with an absolute monarchical tyranny such as that which existed until recently in Russia, then there might be something to be said for the destruction of bourgeois society by any means that would bring it down. Nothing under such conditions could be worse for the mass of the people. But with the destruction of the State in these islands would go the trade unions built up by years of solid labour and sacrifice, the co-operative societies, just now beginning to take a wider outlook on things than mere "divi." hunting, and the democratic political institutions of which the people can make far more use than they do when they choose to exercise their intelligence and bestir their energies. Then the increasingly complicated nature of production, distribution and exchange has also to be considered. A piece of grit will often throw elaborate and delicate machinery out of gear, but we do not regard it as a revolutionary agent on that account. The control of a few engineering workshops by shop stewards, puffed out with vanity and a "little brief authority," will not provide the food necessary to feed the people of these islands. We have, too, an indication of the spirit of liberty with which they are animated in the massed picketing at Glasgow, not against blacklegs and non-unionists, but against fellow trade unionists who refused to aid "unauthorised strikes."

I have said that these "down tools" outbursts are anti-Socialist. They are anti-Socialist because they are anarchical. They may pull down, but they cannot build up. Socialism and Socialists have suffered enough during the war because of the freaks and cranks that the war discovered among us, and the greater number of the same genus who now profess to be Socialists without understanding much, if anything, about the Socialist movement. We do not want further prejudice raised against us by attempts to connect us with anarchical violence, hooliganism and looting. Nothing for the benefit of the people can possibly come out of what is now going on. All it will do is to help reaction, and make even the majority of the working class ready to acquiesce in a mild military dictatorship as a lesser evil than Bolshevist tyranny and violence. And there are some British Generals who are popular, and who are not merely militarists!

There is no royal road to the Social Revolution. The steady and patient work of Socialist propaganda and organisation together with the pressing forward of thorough-going collectivist proposals for the ownership and control of industry for the common good, and the imagination to take advantage of everything that will help forward the great change from capitalist production for profit to Socialist production for use—those are the lines we must follow. All the imaginary shortcuts of the impatient ones, which lead to anarchical deserts or reactionary morasses, serve only to retard real Social-Democratic progress.

Lector House believes that a society develops through a two-fold approach of continuous learning and adaptation, which is derived from the study of classic literary works spread across the historic timeline of literature records. Therefore, we aim at reviving, repairing and redeveloping all those inaccessible or damaged but historically as well as culturally important literature across subjects so that the future generations may have an opportunity to study and learn from past works to embark upon a journey of creating a better future.

This book is a result of an effort made by Lector House towards making a contribution to the preservation and repair of original ancient works which might hold historical significance to the approach of continuous learning across subjects.

HAPPY READING & LEARNING!

LECTOR HOUSE LLP
E-MAIL: lectorpublishing@gmail.com

9 789354 207211